PICKET FENCES
Boundaries for Women

BY CATHY GONZALEZ, PhD

A CHRISTIAN LIVING GUIDE

©revised 2016

Table of Contents

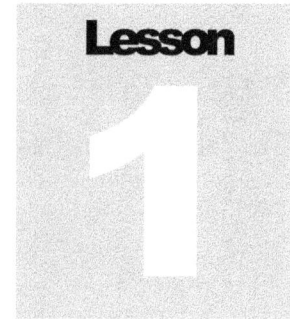

Setting Boundaries God's Way

An overview of the topic o f boundaries based on Biblical principles and examples.

B oundaries define where you end and another person begins. They are not walls. Walls are barriers that restrict and confine a particular space from any other space. An appropriate boundary is a protective, safe space.

Just as a fence in your yard defines your property space, God has also defined who He lets into his "yard". Read the Ten Commandments *Ex 20: 1-17* for examples of appropriate boundaries according to God.

In the past, a fence of upright pointed pickets (pointed stakes often driven into the ground to support a fence) used to be a common site in many American neighborhoods. The pickets were usually spaced at intervals along the fence with spaces in between. The spaces were small enough to prevent intruders slipping through but wide enough to present a friendly, inviting boundary around a yard. The height of picket fences is traditionally high enough to demonstrate a clear boundary but not so high that a person cannot see who ever is on the other side of the fence.

A picket fence around your personal space allows for the flow back and forth of human relations while at the same time protecting the person that God has designed you to be. Your personal picket fence or boundaries keeps you safe without cutting you off from relationship with others in your life.

✝ Visualize a picket fence around the person you are. How high is your fence? How wide apart are the pickets spaced? What does your picture say about how you perceive yourself to be protected or not protected from the influence of others?

What are boundaries?

The following are the primary characteristics of healthy boundaries:

Boundaries define what is "me" and what is "you". By understanding boundaries, you know who "owns" (is responsible) for a particular feeling or attitude.

> *"The heart knows its own bitterness, and its joy no stranger shares."*
> *Proverbs 14:10*

Boundaries help you realize freedom from the sins of self-centeredness, guilt, insecurity, low self-esteem, and the actions of others.

> *"For freedom Christ set us free; so stand firm and do not submit again to the yoke of slavery." Galatians 5:1*

Boundaries offer protection against trespassers by providing a way to protect your soul from evil.

> *"Do not give what is holy to dogs, or throw your pearls before swine, lest they trample them underfoot, and turn and tear you to pieces." Matthew 7: 6*

The nature of God is a perfect testimony to the appropriateness of boundaries. The following verses are examples of God clearly stating who He is.

> *"For I the Lord am your God. You shall make and keep yourselves holy, because I am holy." Leviticus 11:44*

> *"...I will not remain angry with you; For I am merciful, oracle of the Lord, I will not keep my anger forever." Jeremiah 3:12*

> *"Listen to me, Jacob, Israel, whom I called! I, it is I who am the first, and am I the last." Isaiah 48:12*

✦   Discuss some of God's boundaries based on the verses above stating who He is.

Why is a lack of boundaries a problem?

Personal and spiritual conflicts between people are often due to a lack of boundaries. A problem occurs when the owner of a thought or feeling does not take responsibility; for example, Adam blamed Eve → Eve blamed the serpent.

God designed us to have freedom of choice but when we turned from Him, we lost that freedom and sin entered God's original design for life. Mankind become enslaved by:

- Self-centeredness

- Sinful patterns

- Past hurts

- Self-imposed limitations

God gives us words ("I" statements) and God's truth (commandments). When we cross God's commandments, we loose the security that truth provides.

> *"Therefore, putting away falsehood, speak the truth, <u>each one</u> to <u>his</u> neighbor, for we are members one of another." Ephesians 4:25*

> ✍ Rewrite Ephesians 4:25 as an "I" statement (the words to change are underlined in the scripture quote above).

> _____

> _____

> _____

The boundary Paul was trying to teach the church at Ephesus was not to allow dishonesty into their "yard". The pickets on your fence are to be guardians of truth. Living in a sinful world, we can often be deceived. By deceiving someone else, we can actually bring harm to ourselves because it gives Satan a foothold into our minds and hearts. This boundary considers the good of both the other person and yourself.

If you aren't truthful with the other person, the real relationship goes into hiding. People in denial are deaf to words of truth; they only respond to pain and loss.

What does a healthy boundary look like?

Setting boundaries is actually growing in character which means boundaries are healthy and positive.

None of us are perfect but we can try hard to establish healthy boundaries. Someone that is working at establishing healthy boundaries does the following:

Practices self-control -- you cannot fix or control someone else so you must learn self-control.

> *"In contrast, the fruit of the Spirit is love, joy, peace, patience, kindness, generosity, faithfulness, gentleness, self-control. Against such there is no law."*
>
> *Galatians 5:22-23*

✝ Do you tend to focus on what the other person needs to change?

Accepts responsibility -- responsibility involves action. You can participate in the resolution of conflict even if it is not because of your own fault. Instead of reacting, learn to think through your choices.

> *"A city breached and left defenseless are those who do not control their temper."*
>
> *Proverbs 25:28*

✝ Do you often use the terms "I had to" or "he/she made me"?

Owns feelings – emotions are signals that alert you to be aware of the condition of your heart. Accepting feelings as your own property motivates you to do much good or to seek God's will. To choose to take responsibility bears the fruit of self-control.

> *"At the sight of the crowds, his heart was moved with pity for them because they were*
>
> *troubled and abandoned, like sheep without a shepherd." Matthew 9:36*

Consider what you tend to do with your feelings. Look at any problem that needs to be addressed.

> *"Each must do as already determined, without sadness or compulsion, for God loves*
>
> *a cheerful giver." 2 Corinthians 9:7*

✝ Do you often begin a sentence with "You made me feel ……"?

Reflects thoughtfully – clarifies any distorted ideas. Considering past relationships in their proper context shows us if we are reacting to feelings of what has happened in the past. It makes us realize that was then and this is now.

> *"...take every thought captive in obedience to Christ...."*   2
>
> *Corinthians 10:5*

✝ Are your feelings appropriate for what is going on now?

Seeks God's desire – feeling unsatisfied results from seeking your desires from others instead of from God. Desires often go unsatisfied because you lack the internal structure of appropriate boundaries that enable you to define and take specific action to reach your goals.

> *"The Lord watches over all who love him…" Psalms 145:20*

✝ Do you trust God can meet any of your needs?

If you have tried to be adaptive, loving and avoid conflict but the other person uses that as permission to be unloving, give the other person a choice to own their problem or physically place a boundary (we will discuss abusive relationships in another lesson).

A person with good boundary skills does not set boundaries on someone else. You should only set boundaries on yourself because you can only control yourself.

A good question to ask of yourself is "Am I trying to control the other person by setting this boundary?"

Handling Boundary Myths

The Bible clearly tells us what are healthy boundaries but our family or past relationships confuse how we believe. We have to reconcile the lies the world has told us with God's Biblical truths. A few examples are:

1. **Myth – "I'm being selfish."**

   Being selfish is defined as being fixated on your own wishes and desires to the exclusion of any responsibility to be loving towards others.

   "In vain do they worship me, teaching as doctrines human precepts. You

   disregard God's commandment but cling to human tradition." Mark 7:7-8

   God's Truth – "My needs are my responsibility."

   God has given us the Holy Spirit as a counselor and guide for help in making healthy and unselfish decisions.

   "Therefore, we aspire to please him, whether we are at home or away."

   2 Corinthians 5:9

2. Myth – "Setting boundaries is a sign of disobedience."

   Read *Matthew 19:16-22.*

   Jesus let the ruler go because he did not want to comply with God's boundaries so Jesus did not manipulate him into compliance. If someone does not respect your boundary, gain support from God and support persons who are Biblically-sound believers too.

   God's Truth – "A lack of boundaries is often a sign you are doing a good thing for a bad reason or saying yes because you are afraid to say no."

   It is a type of lie when you say "yes" to God or someone else when you really mean "no". You can say "no" to good things for wrong reasons but setting a boundary helps you to clarify, to be honest, and to recognize the truth about your motives. Having a clear conscience, you then can allow God to work in you.

3. **Myth -- Setting a boundary hurts others.**

"Appropriate boundaries don't control, attack, or hurt anyone. They simply prevent your treasures from being taken at the wrong time. This principle speaks not only to those who would like to control or manipulate us, but it also applies to the legitimate needs of others." (Cloud, Boundaries: When to Say YES, When to Say NO, To Take Control of Your Life, 1992)

God's Truth -- Boundaries are defensive tools, not offensive.

> *"[22]Then he made the disciples get into the boat and precede him to the other side, while he dismissed the crowds. [23]After doing so, he went up on the mountain by himself to pray." Matthew 14:22-23*

4. **Myth -- Setting a boundary makes others mad and hurts me.**

The world (Satan in particular) wants us to live our lives trying to please others or ourselves all the time rather than pleasing God. Being a people pleaser does more harm than good.

God's Truth – Boundaries help us set appropriate limits.

Paul set limits on the Corinthians' rebellion even though the Corinthians did not like it!

> *"[8]For even if I saddened you by my letter, I do not regret it; and if I did regret it ([for] I see that that letter saddened you, if only for a while), [9]I rejoice now, not because you were saddened, but because you were saddened into repentance; for you were saddened in a godly way, so that you did not suffer loss in anything because of us." 2 Corinthians 7:8-9.*

5. **Myth -- Setting a boundary makes me feel guilty.**

Guilt results from our feelings of obligation. We consider the love, money, or time we have received from others is a debt we must repay rather than a gift we have received.

God's Truth -- Don't confuse boundaries and gifts.

We owe thanks to God more so than to others. In response to our grateful heart, we then go and help others.

Types of healthy boundaries

Physical boundaries are different from boundaries dealing with our soul and emotional relationships.

Emotional distance is sometimes an appropriate or inappropriate boundary depending on your motivation.

Physical distance can also be appropriate or inappropriate. It is appropriate if it provides time to protect, think, heal, and learn new things.

> *"The astute see an evil and hide; the naïve continue on and pay the penalty."*
>
> *Proverbs 27:12*

Examples of physical distance are:

- Taking a physical timeout in another room

- Extended timeout to sort things out

- Moving out to get treatment for an addiction

- Moving to a shelter to protect yourself and/or children

Physical distance is inappropriate if we are using it instead of trusting God or in an attempt to control a situation. (We will discuss this in relationship to abusive situations later in this study.)

"Boundaries are only built and established in the context of relationship. To run from a relationship as the first step of boundaries is not to have boundaries at all. It is a defense against developing boundaries with another person." (Cloud, Boundaries in Marriage, 2002)

Search your motives for establishing boundaries to make sure that they are motivated by love and not due to revenge, feeling superior spiritually, or self-pity.

The best way to set healthy boundaries is to make God part of the process. We do this by:

- Being educated about the risk of setting a boundary and being prepared. We live in a fallen world and are under attack by Satan.

   "In fact, all who want to live religiously in Christ Jesus will be persecuted."
   2 Timothy 3:12

- Follow Peter's example by fixing your eyes on Jesus.

   "He said, "Come." Peter got out of the boat and began to walk on the water toward Jesus." Matthew 14:29

- Look to Jesus for help.

   "Who trained my hands for war, my arms to string a bow of bronze."
   Psalm 18:35

- Believe 100 percent that Jesus will be there to match your efforts.

✦ Read Matthew 7:24-27. Discuss how this passage relates to setting healthy boundaries.

📖 Begin keeping a daily journal about boundaries. In your journal, record a specific boundary you are struggling with. Pray the Boundaries Prayer each day. Be on the lookout for answers to your boundary issue and record how God responds in your journal. Bring your journal to the next study if you would like to share with the rest of the group.

Boundaries Prayer

God, you now where I am on this journey toward healthy boundaries. I thank you for the emotions you built into me to warn me of boundary violations. Teach me to pay attention to those internal signals. Open my eyes to the boundary-lovers around me and help me to learn from them. Thank you for the blessing of supportive people and the valuable lessons and love these people offer me. And thank you for your love and for the worth I can find in you, despite childhood lessons I learned about my lack of worth.

Give me courage to practice my no's and give me wisdom as I choose people to practice with. Thank you that I can rejoice in my guilt, knowing that your rules for living are better than the negative rules that I learned growing up, the rules that generate these messages of guilt. Give me courage to confront the boundary-busters in my life with grownup no's.

Thank you for the knowledge that someday the guilt will be gone and for that sign of health, that sign of your loving and healing faithfulness in my life. Teach me to love others as myself and to respect their boundaries the way I want them to respect mine. And teach me to count the cost when I see an opportunity to give, and then to freely say yes or just as freely say no.

Finally, it is my prayer that you will continue to help me learn to take ownership of my life, to teach me to see what is my responsibility and what isn't, to show me what problems I've taken on that you never intended for me, and to guide me as I try to establish and live by biblical boundaries. May I live a life of love, freedom, responsibility, and service to your glory. I pray in Jesus' name. Amen.

Adapted from (Cloud, Boundaries: When to Say YES, When to Say NO, To Take Control of Your Life, 1992)

Dealing with Male Relationships

Dealing with love relationships in dating and marriage.

God cares deeply about women's love relationships with men. God cares deeply about marriage! As marriages break, people desperately need God's directions for living with a partner in marriage.

The first time God is referred to as the Lord God is when He prepares a place for man to live in and establishes the home. He Himself was the first Homemaker — which in itself holds the key to mending broken homes and broken families.

In Genesis 1:1 the Hebrew word Elohim is used for God. His name is revealed as Jehovah Elohim, which translates as "Lord God" in Chapter 2. Jehovah Elohim implies the concept of God revealing Himself to his people in a personal way. The first time God revealed Himself personally was in a home.

In the beginning Adam was single and lonely. The primary reason for the woman's creation was not to produce children or provide sexual satisfaction or to keep the home but for the **mutual happiness** of the man and woman. The fact that Eve was created after Adam or that she was his designated companion and helper does not mean she was in any way inferior to Adam. As his partner, she was his equal.

✦ Read 1 Peter 3:7 -- the New Testament reaffirms the principle of equality when it says men and women are *"joint heirs of the gift of life…"*. Discuss what it means to be an "heir together".

The apostle Paul, whose views of women are often misunderstood and misquoted, said in Galatians:

> *"There is neither Jew nor Greek, there is neither slave nor free person, there is*
>
> *not male and female; for you are one in Christ Jesus." Gal 3:28*

Much marital brokenness is the result of not understanding the psychological commitment of mutual happiness.

"That is why a man leaves his father and mother and clings to his wife, and the two of them become one body." Genesis 2:24

The becoming one is physical, sexual. It has nothing to do with one spouse having control over another spouse's mind or emotions.

Unevenly Yoked

Saint Paul teaches about the problems of Christians who are in relationships with unbelievers. He is concerned that these relationships are detrimental and he encourages us to avoid them. Is he right to do so? Is Saint Paul a male chauvinist, or has he actually got it right?

A generation that bases every criterion for good on what one "feels", rather than on what is objectively good, might easily think so. Compromise has long been a problem for Christians who have formed intimate relationships with unbelievers. In some cases, their marriages have turned out well in spite of this. Others that also began with a beautiful romance full of dreams, have turned out disastrous: They have ended in frustration, painful divorce and alienation from their church fellowship and the Sacraments. Not to mention the devastating effect on the moral and emotional health of the children.

To be unequally yoked with a nonbeliever can happen in a Christian relationship as well. **This happens when one partner, although baptized, does not believe in, nor practice their faith.** Sadly, the results can be the same although a Christian marriage has taken place. Even where marriages have not broken up, there is still pain and loneliness for the believing spouse. They cannot share that part of their life with the one they love most. Many settle for compromise, trying not to talk or argue about religion. Both partners can form separate relationships with like-minded people which can, and often do, become a source of jealousy, frustration and competition for them both.

The problem with being unequally yoked is that a woman must constantly try to balance her life between two "lords". This leads to a continual compromise of her faith and the dilution of God's principles in her family so that God is not taken seriously in daily, practical matters.

✝ How do you know if your man is leaving God out? Use the following checklist:

☐ Out of decisions	☐ Out of activities
☐ Out of business	☐ Out of the home
☐ Out of female relationships	☐ Out of leisure time
☐ Out of financial plans	☐ Out of life

In the series of books on Boundaries written by Drs. Cloud and Townsend, they define certain key boundary laws. Let's look at how these apply to marriage.

The Law of Sowing and Reaping

The law of cause and effect is a basic law of life. The Bible calls it the Law of Sowing and Reaping. When God tells us that we will reap what we sow, He is not punishing us; He's telling us how things really are.

"Make no mistake: God is not mocked, for a person will reap only what he sows, because the one who sows for his flesh will reap corruption from the flesh, but the one who sows for the spirit will reap eternal life from the spirit." Galatians 6:7-8

✠ Life is not always fair. Where does Paul promise we will "reap"?

The Law of Responsibility

Problems arise when boundaries of responsibility are confused. **We are to love one another, not be one another!** You can't feel, think, be spiritual, behave, work through feelings, or grow for someone else. You can only do this for yourself.

"So then, my beloved, obedient as you have always been, not only when I am present but all the more now when I am absent, work out your salvation with fear and trembling. God God is the one who, for his good purpose, works in you both to desire and to work." Philippians 2:12-13

✦ What does Philippians 2:12-13 say about managing your personal growth?

✠ Where are you getting angry, pouting, and acting disappointed in hopes of controlling your partner?

✠ Where are you giving in to your partner's anger, pouting, and disappointments and, thereby, taking responsibility for what he is feeling?

How we are to respond to people whose boundaries are not well defined?

"Do to others whatever you would have them do to you." Matthew 7:12

Law of Power

Accepting someone as they are, respecting their choice to be that way, and giving appropriate consequences means we execute the power we do have and stop trying to exert the power no one has.

Give up trying to have control and power over your partner.

> *"...gentleness and self-control. Against such things there is no law."* Gal 5:23

✦ What do you think about exercising the Law of Power?

✝ What consequences might your partner experience?

✝ Do you believe these consequences can prompt the change that your nagging won't?

Law of Evaluation

We should not establish boundaries simply by looking at the effect it has on ourselves. Be responsible to your partner, in addition to yourself, by evaluating the effects of setting a boundary.

We need to be honest with one another about how we are hurt.

> *"Therefore, putting away falsehood, speak the truth, each one to his neighbor, for we are members one of another."* Ephesians 4:25

✝ Which of your behaviors will the Law of Evaluation force you to become responsible for?

✝ What boundaries of your partner do you need to respect more?

The Law of Exposure

Your boundaries need to be made visible to your partner and communicated in your relationship.

Many boundary problems result from relational fears such as fear of guilt, not being liked, loss of love, loss of connection, loss of approval, receiving anger, or being known. We try to have secret boundaries because of these fears.

Have you ever been told "I can't read your mind!" The Biblical mandate is to be honest and be in the light.

"13But everything exposed by the light becomes visible, for everything that becomes visible is light. 14Therefore, it says: "Awake, O sleeper, and arise from the dead, and Christ will give you light." Ephesians 5:13-14

✟ Do you need to work on owning your feelings and hurts, and lovingly communicate them to your partner?

✟ Do you remove yourself from injurious situations in the relationship to protect your treasures?

✟ When you need time away, do you let your partner know he is experiencing the consequences of his out-of-control behavior (Matthew 18:17, 1 Corinthians 5:9-13) or do you let your partner guess?

✟ What will you say the next time you need space?

Codependency

When one person becomes dependent upon another person for emotional survival, she is at the mercy of the man who can meet those needs. A woman should complete a man; our differences are intended to complement and complete each other.

An aspect of completing includes accountability. This leads to trust.

"Two are better than one: They get a good wage for their toil. If the one falls, the other will help the fallen one. But woe to the solitary person! If that one should fall, there is no other to help." Ecclesiastes 4: 9-10

The Dreaded "S" Word – Submission

✍ Write down what your current concept of submission in marriage:

_____

_____

_____

_____

Men and women uniquely express aspects of God's character through their ability to choose, their eternal souls, and their creative abilities. Christ's ministry on earth clearly demonstrated the value that He placed on women. He treated women with even greater dignity than His culture demanded.

Submission in marriage does not mean that a woman should not share her opinions. Most women don't want to have their own way so much as they want to be heard and valued for their knowledge and opinion.

Abraham's wife, Sarah was a submissive wife.

"[5]For this is how the holy women who hoped in God once used to adorn themselves and were subordinate to their husbands; [6]thus Sarah obeyed Abraham, calling him "lord." You are her children when do what is good and fear no intimidation."
1 Peter 3:5-6

Sarah clearly played an active role in her home. She respected Abraham and gave him the final authority to make decisions but she did not withhold her feelings and opinions. In one instance, God actually encouraged Abraham to listen to her.

"[10]So she demanded of Abraham: "Drive out that slave and her son! No son of that slave is going to share the inheritance with my son Isaac!" [11]Abraham was greatly distressed because it concerned a son of his. [12]But God said to Abraham: Do not be distressed about the boy or about your slave woman. Obey Sarah, no matter what she asks of you; for it is through Isaac that descendants will bear your name."
Genesis 21:10-12

Submission does not mean blind obedience. The Greek words for "obey" and "submit" are different and communicate subtly different messages. The word translated as "obey" is used to describe the relationship between children and their parents. To obey means to listen and act without questioning the recognized authority.

Submission is a willing act of placing oneself under the authority of another. Christ is our perfect example of submission. He willingly submitted His desire to His Father's authority by coming to earth, suffering and dying on the cross.

The command to submit to your husband does not mean that a woman should turn her brain off. She willingly and thoughtfully commits to giving him a place of leadership; however, she can and should reason with him if he is making decisions that seem to contradict what she understands the Bible to say is moral, correct and wise.

Greek for submission is *hupotasso* (a voluntary attitude of giving in and cooperating). Supporting and cooperating means that you have to let go of always making the right decision and focus on building the right relationship.

The following discussion on submission is how it relates to a marriage between two believers. It can also relate to a marriage where the husband is not a believer and there is an absence of mental, emotional, or physical abuse. We will cover how submission relates in abusive relationships in the last chapter.

"Wives and Husbands. Be subordinate to one another out of reverence for Christ."

Ephesians 5:21

✦ What does Ephesians 5:21 mean to you?

Many men and women struggle with the advice Paul gives. What Paul is saying is that in any human relationship – husband and wife, child and parent, slave and master – a third party is involved. That third party is Christ! Paul urges us to conduct those relationships in light of Christ's own spirit.

Let's look at several examples of how submission works.

- Sometimes submission in marriage means we don't get our own way even though we believe with certainty that we are correct. Letting a loved one suffer consequences turns into a growing experience. We trust God and obey Him by submitting and leaving the outcome in His hands.

  "Son though he was, he learned obedience from what he suffered;" Hebrews 5:8

- Submitting to your husband is a sign of respect and demonstrates trust towards him and God.

  "As the church is subordinate to Christ, so wives should be subordinate to their husbands in everything." Ephesians 5:24

- Husbands have an equal role to fill in a submissive Christian marriage.

  "25Husbands, love your wives, even as Christ loved the church and handed himself over for her 26to sanctify her, cleansing her by the bath of water with the word, 27that he might present to himself the church in splendor, without spot or wrinkle or any such thing, that she might be holy and without blemish." Ephesians 5:25-27

✍ What picture of submission does Paul teach us in Ephesians 5:24-27?

✍

✍

✍ Paul is showing us that this is not a one-sided submission, but a reciprocal love relationship.

Even though these passages have been misinterpreted and changed to mean a woman should do whatever her husband says, Paul never intended that meaning. In reality, he was saying the husband had the tougher job in submission. Not only is this sacrificing an expression of our Lord's love, but also an example of how the husband ought to devote himself to his wife's good. To give oneself up to death for the beloved is a more extreme expression of devotion than the wife is called on to make.

The Biblical Marriage Model

The Bible says that in a Christian marriage each partner has a unique role that the other cannot fill. Marriage is modeled by Christ's relationship with His church on earth.

	Unique Roles
Christ	Died for ours sins
Church	Represents Christ on earth; obeys His commandments
Man	Provides a male role model to children
Woman	Gives birth to children

Men and women also share some of the same qualities. Both have the following in common:

1. Abilities (can be negotiated)

2. Interests (uniqueness)

3. Personhood (soul)

4. Feelings/desires (a want or expectation; problem lies in who is responsible for the want; no bad person, only conflicting wants; could argue all day about who is being selfish and you get no where!)

5. Attitudes

6. Behaviors

7. Choices

8. Values

Submission is a choice. Christ chose to submit to His father's will out of love; you also can choose to submit in your marriage out of love for God and your spouse.

Do you believe you have free choice or do you believe you are "under the law"? The Bible promises that those who are under the law will experience feelings of anger, guilt, insecurity, and alienation.

> *"You are separated from Christ, you who are trying to be justified by law; you have*
>
> *fallen from grace." Galatians 5:4*

Be aware when you give past the love point to the resentment point.

> *"Each must do as already determined, without sadness or compulsion, for God loves*
>
> *a cheerful giver." 2 Corinthians 9:7*

✝ Where do you need to set some limits on what you will give?

✝ Where do you need to take responsibility for your own wants instead of expecting your husband to provide them?

The following actions will help you and your spouse toward personal change in a marital relationship. Remember you can only control your actions. You can discuss these steps but it is up to him to choose what he is willing to do and it is up to you choose what you are willing to do.

1. Inventory the Symptom

    a. Determine what is the problem.

    b. Do you both agree to take action to solve it?

2. Identify the Specific Boundary Problem

    a. Identify what boundary issue is behind the symptom you identified.

    b. Who is having trouble saying no; who is having trouble hearing no?

3. Find the Origins of the Conflict

    a. Reflect on what you experienced and learned in your family of origin that you are now transferring to your marriage.

    b.   Honestly look at your fears, expectations, self-doubts -- are any of these affecting how you relate to your partner?

4. Take in the Good

    a.   Review what support system is offering you the strength you need as you learn to set boundaries.

    b.   Where can you go for help if you need it?

5. Practice boundary setting with safe people first

    a.   Decide who are safe people with whom you can practice your new boundaries

    b.   When will you tell one of them "no," share an opinion that is different, give something without expecting anything in return?

6. Say No to the Bad

    a.   Seek help to determine if your situation is an abusive one or there are unreasonable demands being made by your spouse.

    b.   Remember the parable of the talents (Matthew 25:14-30), there is no growth without risk and facing up to fear.

7. Forgive

    a.   Unforgiving people allow other people to control them.

    b.   Are you being unforgiving?

8. Become Proactive

    a.   Set some boundaries instead of letting your spouse be in control in a negative way.

    b.   What do you want to do?

    c.   What will you do to reach that goal?

    d.   What will your limits be in the out-of-control areas of your relationships?

    e.   What will you no longer allow yourself to be a party to?

    f.   What will you no longer tolerate?

    g.   What consequences will you set?

9. Learn to live in freedom and responsibility

    a. Where are you still giving out of a sense of guilt and obligation, out of a self-centeredness that hopes to receive in return, out of compliance because of poor boundaries?

    b. To whom can you give something (be specific) simply because you want to.

📖 Write a prayer for your partner in your journal and pray it every day this week.

The little things are the big things.
It is never being too old to hold hands.
It is remembering to say
"I love you" at least once a day.
It is never going to sleep angry.

It is at no time taking the other for granted;
The courtship should not end with the honeymoon,
it should continue through all the years.

It is having a mutual sense of values and common objectives.
It is standing together facing the world.
It is forming a circle of love that gathers in the whole family.
It is doing things for each other, not in the attitude
of duty or sacrifice, but in the spirit of joy.

It is speaking words of appreciation and
Demonstrating gratitude in thoughtful ways.
It is not expecting the husband to wear a halo
or the wife to have wings of an angel.

It is not looking for perfection in each other.
It is cultivating flexibility, patience,
understanding and a sense of humor.

It is having the capacity to forgive and forget.
It is giving each other an atmosphere in which each can grow.
It is finding room for the things of the spirit.
It is a common search for the good and the beautiful.

It is establishing a relationship in which the independence is equal,
Dependence is mutual and the obligation is reciprocal.
It is not only marrying the right partner,
it is being the right partner.

Building Loving Boundaries with Children

Dealing with relationships with children, teens, and adult children.

The family is the social unit God invented to fill up the world with representatives of his loving character. The church is a great example:

"So therefore, while we have the opportunity, let us do good to all, but especially to those who belong to the __family__ of the faith." Galatians 6:10

What do the following verses say about the family of God?

"So then you are no longer strangers and sojourners, but you are fellow citizens with the holy ones and members of the household of God,...." Ephesians 2:19

"But if I should be delayed, you should know how to behave in the household of God, which is the church of the living God, the pillar and foundation of truth." 1 Timothy 4:15

✎ What are some of the examples of family we see in our lives today that are different from the typical mother/father scenario? Does God consider these valid families? Explain your answer.

_____

—

"Of all the areas in which boundaries are crucial, none is more relevant than that of raising children. How we approach boundaries and child rearing will have enormous impact on the characters of our kids—how they develop values, how well they do in school, what friends they pick, whom they marry, and how well they do in a career." (Cloud, Boundaries: When to Say YES, When to Say NO, To Take Control of Your Life, 1992)

Boundaries and Responsibility

Next to the parent-child bonding relationship, the most important job an adult has in the family unit is teaching the children responsibility. This includes the children understanding what they are responsible for and what they are **not** responsible for, knowing how to say no and how to accept someone else's no.

God as our parent is the role model from which we learn to accept responsibility.

> *...until we all attain to the unity of faith and knowledge of the Son of God, to mature manhood, to the extent of the full stature of Christ." Ephesians 4:13*

✦ What did you learn about boundaries when you were a child? Did you learn to hate them, fear them, respect them, and/or develop them?

✞ How do you respond when others set limits on you? Do you have a tantrum or sulk? Do you comply in order to keep the peace?

✞ Do you see any parallels between your answer to question 1 and question 2?

Boundaries and Discipline versus Punishment

✍ Take a moment and write down your own personal definition of **discipline**:

_____

_____

_____

✍ Take a moment and write down your own personal definition of **punishment**:

_____

_____

_____

Compare your definitions with the chart below:

Punishment	Discipline
1. Payment for wrongdoing	1. External boundary designed to develop internal boundaries
2. Leaves little room for practice/mistakes	2. In Greek and Hebrew means "teaching"
3. God has already punished us; Christ's suffering paid for our wrongdoing	3. Natural law of God; our actions reap consequences
4. Causes us to comply without learning	4. Frees us to make mistakes without fear of judgment
5. Looks back in time	5. Looks forward in time

There are positive and negative aspects of discipline:

- **Positive discipline** is educating and training a child to do a task.
- **Negative discipline** is letting the child suffer the results of their actions to learn a lesson in responsibility.

Positive Discipline Aspects	Negative Discipline Aspects
proactive	correction
prevention	chastisement

✦ Think of a specific example of punishment from your childhood and share how it worked based on the definitions we have looked at in this chapter.

✦ How would you redo this with your child to make it a discipline rather than a punishment?

✝ What does it mean to you that God will not judge you or withdraw his love from you? How can you let your children know that you will not judge them or withdraw your love from them?

Tie consequences as closely as possible to the action of the child. This is particularly important for children with mental challenges who have limited reasoning or memory retention ability. I call this "carrots before dessert" discipline.

If consequences for little things are the same as for big things, severe consequences become meaningless.

Allowing Children to Have a Sense of Control and Choice

Learning to make age-appropriate choices helps children develop a sense of security and control in their lives. By children learning that their destiny is largely theirs to determine, they are trained to weigh choices rather than avoid taking responsibility for decision-making.

> "I won't go to the dentist—you can't make me go!" Pamela stamped her eleven-year-old feet and scowled at her father, Sal, who was waiting at the front door.
>
> There had been a time when Sal would have reacted in a knee-jerk fashion to Pamela's power move. He would have said something like, "Well, we'll see about that!" and physically dragged the screaming child into the car.
>
> However, lots of family counseling and reading up on these issues had prepared Sal for the inevitable. Calmly he said to her, "You're absolutely right, Honey. I can't make you go to the dentist. If you don't want to go, you don't have to. But remember our rule: if you choose not to go, you're also choosing not to go to the party tomorrow night. I'll certainly respect either decision. Shall I cancel your appointment?"
>
> Pamela looked perplexed and though a minute. Then, slowly, she replied, "I'll go. But I'm not going because I have to." Pamela was right. She was choosing to go to her appointment because she wanted to attend the party.
>
> Children need to have a sense of control and choice in their lives. They need to see themselves not as the dependent, helpless pawns of parents, but as choosing, willing, initiative-taking agents of their own lives.

What do you like about the way Sal dealt with Pamela's objection to going to the dentist? What, if anything, did not you like?

Refer back to the Positive/Negative Aspects of Discipline list and identify the aspect Sal used with Pamela. What might have happened if Sal had demanded Pamela comply with his request?

What happens when adults make their children's choices for them and try to prevent them from making painful decisions?

Delaying Gratification of Goals

Kids these days want everything "now"! Delaying gratification means a child has the ability to say "no" to their impulses, wishes, and desires until later in life.

God uses the concept of delayed gratification to help His children see the benefits of planning and preparing.

> *"...For the sake of the joy that lay before him he endured the cross, despising its shame, and has taken his seat at the right of the throne of God."* Hebrews 12:2

> ✍ What does the above verse tell us about delayed gratification? What did Jesus gain from this? _____

Read Proverbs 6: 6-11. This is a great lesson about the lowly ant for teens and grown children who are not motivated.

> *"⁶Go to the ant, O sluggard, study her ways and learn wisdom; ⁷For though she has no chief, no commander or ruler, ⁸She procures her food in the summer, stores up her provisions in the harvest. ⁹How long, O sluggard, will you lie there? When will you rise from your sleep? ¹⁰A little sleep, a little slumber, a little folding of the arms to rest—¹¹Then poverty will come upon you like a robber, and want like a brigand."*

Learning how to delay gratification helps children and teens develop a goal orientation.

> *"Which of you wishing to construct a tower does not first sit down and calculate the cost to see if there is enough for its completion?"* Luke 14:28

✝ What benefits do you see in teaching the delay of gratification to your children?

✝ How did you learn—or how are you learning—the value of delaying gratification?

Respecting the Limits of Others

If we do not teach children to accept someone else's "no", someone who loves them far less may take on the job.

Learning to accept the limits of others is important because it helps the child love in a Christ-like manner. This lesson can keep our children from being self-centered or controlling adults.

✦   How can we teach our children in a positive way that their actions matter?

Avoiding Clinging to Children

In her devotional book, *Jesus Calling*, Sarah Young writes about entrusting our loved ones to Christ's loving care. Often with children, parents can cling too tightly to their children. If you let a child become an idol of your heart, you endanger them as well as yourself. The story of Joseph and his father, Jacob, found in the Bible tells the story of a parent who favored his one child over all the others. Joseph's brothers came to hate him and sold him off into slavery. Eventually the family was reconciled with one another but not before years of suffering and separation occurred.

Sarah Young writes that when you release your loved ones to Christ, you are entrusting them to Him so they can receive His blessings. This frees you up to "cling to" His hand. (Young, 2004)

Dealing with Adult Children

There are no guarantees that training will be heeded. Once children become adults (after no longer financially depending on you which varies depending on college aspirations,) they are no longer under authority to their parents.

Children have the responsibility to listen and learn during childhood. Even if you made mistakes, remember you were doing the best you could at the time. Forgive yourself for the past and look to today because that is what God does for us.

"Lord, you are good and forgiving, most merciful to all who call on you." Psalm 86:5

Influences from the outside world can negate many good efforts made by good parents.

✎   What influences can you identify that can negatively impact our adult children?

✎

The following are some helping strategies with adult children:

- ✠ Seek the peace of God in your heart in order to have the peace of God in your relationship with your child.

- ✠ Have a home that exalts God; do not compromise your home style to make the adult child comfortable.

- ✠ Establish communication rules that are equitable, reasonable, and "keepable."

- ✠ Be as flexible as you can where the child's identity, independence and self-esteem are concerned. Give lots of support and encouragement.

- ✠ Provide as much stability and Christian example in your life as you can.

- ✠ Be predictable in your moods and monitor your emotions.

- ✠ Do not be afraid to show physical affection but be mindful of asking permission with a child who shies away from this type of affection.

- ✠ Do not show up unannounced at your child's home. Try to allow them to make the majority of contact.

- ✠ Spend time talking with your adult child. Ask them questions that will allow them to express their feelings about situations as they grew up. Caution: be willing to passively listen and not be judgmental before initiating these conversations. Even if you don't agree, you can still affirm the child:

    a. I respect your opinion on this;

    b. I do not remember the incidents exactly like you do but I believe you remember it that way and that is good enough for me;

    c. I apologize for letting you down/not being there for you; will you forgive me;

    d. I can hear how hurt you were about this incident.

    e. Do not tell your adult child how they should act! Talk to God about it, not the kid.

Sometimes, no matter how hard we try, focusing on prayer gets difficult if not impossible. Stress over adult children who have fallen in grace is one of those particularly hard times. When this happens to you, try using a guideword—like the word "Father' – and relate your specific prayer concern to each letter. For instance, say you're praying for a child who has lost his faith:

F is for faith. *Lord, I firmly believe in your love and power and I believe you will bring my child back to your fold.*

A is for adoration. *I adore you as the God who gave life to me and to my child, the God who loves me even if I haven't been a perfect parent, and who loves my child even though he has sinned.*

T is for thanksgiving. *Father, I thank you every day for this child, for the gift of his life.*

H is for humility. *Lord, I've lost my way, too. I can't reach my child. Only with your help will I know how to handle this problem.*

E is for entreaty. *Heavenly Father, you promised your son anything we ask in His name will be granted. I beseech you, as Father to thy son and Father to us all, please bring my child back.*

R is for resolution. *Lord, I place this problem in Your hands. I resolve to accept my child as he is, not as I wish him to be. I resolve not to turn away from him, but with Your help, I will find a way to reach him.*

Special Needs Children

Safe-suffering means learning from age appropriate consequences. With special needs children, age appropriateness does not necessarily mean the same as for children without physical or mental challenges.

Provide opportunities for siblings to have a safe method for communicating honest feelings about their challenged brother or sister. Safe zones are necessary for effective communication. A safe zone is:

1. Private and away from the challenged family member – this allows the sibling to say honestly what they think without fear of hurting someone's feelings.

2. Spend recreational time with the siblings without the special needs child being present. This gives quality time without uncontrollable interruptions.

3. When a sibling wants time to talk with a parent but that is impossible because of the special needs child, say "What you want to say is very important to me and I want to give you my full attention. Because I cannot do that right now, let's talk …..(set specific time and place)." Then do everything you can to keep your appointment.

4. Whenever you have to go to extreme measures to control or discipline your special needs child, it may appear as uncaring behavior on your part and be interpreted as mean or cruel in the eyes of siblings, particularly younger siblings. After things calm down, find an opportunity away from the special needs child to explain in age appropriate language exactly what was going on and why you acted as you did.

5. Once a week, have 30 minutes of family prayer time. "The family that prays together, stays together!" Pick one simple Bible verse the day before and ask the children to prepare something for prayer time that demonstrates what the verse means to them. Have the kids include their special needs sibling in whatever they chose to do. Provide puppets or costume materials. Tell the kids they have 3 minutes to show what the verse means. Then have prayer time together.

For adult special needs children, do what is best for them and know you have God's blessing. Remember they have a life to lead that God has planned for them just as all God's children do.

📖 Pick one child relationship that you are struggling with and write a prayer for that person each day in your journal for a week. As each day goes by, record after your prayer how you are feeling. At the end of the week, read what you have been writing, pay particular attention to how your feelings change.

Growing Healthy Relationships with Relatives

Dealing with relationships in your external family

I n the book <u>Boundaries</u>, Drs. Cloud and Townsend write "People who own their lives do not feel guilty when they make choices about where they are going." (Cloud, Boundaries: When to Say YES, When to Say NO, To Take Control of Your Life, 1992)

Your Family of Origin

Your family of origin is your external family. This includes parents, siblings, grandparents, aunts, uncles, cousins, and any step-family members.

Family members have the power to affect your current life in a trickle-down effect. One sure sign of this is when your relationships with a member of your family have the power to affect your relationships with others.

✝ Do you feel guilty about certain choices you have made?
What guides the decisions you make?
Do you choose out of love or guilt?

See if you can identify your family from the following categories described in the book, <u>Boundaries</u> (Cloud, Boundaries: When to Say YES, When to Say NO, To Take Control of Your Life, 1992):

Catching the Virus

Your family of origin has the power to affect your new family in a trickle-down effect.

Second Fiddle

Your current relationships always take a backseat to the relationships with your family of origin.

May I Have My Allowance, Please?

There is financial dependency between your current family or spouse's family, or you are an adult still financially or emotionally dependent on your family of origin.

Mom, where are my Socks?

You are an adult whose family of origin performs certain life management functions (hangs out at parents' house constantly, vacations with parents exclusively, usually eats/does laundry at parents' home) and does not have functional adult relationships with friends.

The Dilemma of Triangulation

In a triangulation, people speak falsely, fail to own their own anger, put on false fronts (cover up feelings with nice words and flattery), and gossip (erodes relationships).

> *"Therefore, putting away falsehood, speak the truth, each one to his neighbor, for we are members one of another."* Ephesians 4:25

Triangulation Model

B talks to A

A talks to C

C talks to B

A talks to B.........

A

B

C

What does the Bible teach in the following passages in relationship to triangulation?

"You shall not hate any of your kindred in your heart..." Leviticus 19:17

_____

_____

"Whoever rebukes another wins more favor than one who flatters with the tongue." Proverbs 28:23

_____

_____

"Therefore, if you bring your gift to the alter, and there recall that your brother has anything against you, leave your gift there at the altar, go first and be reconciled with your brother, and then com and offer your gift." Matthew 5:23-24

_____

_____

Caring for Elderly Parents

The Bible teaches that adult children should help care for their elderly parents.
See 1 Timothy 5:3-4.

Two problems may sometimes come up, however, that make this teaching difficult to follow:

- Parents aren't really in need but act demanding or like martyrs.

- Parents need care but you are not able to face/deal with the situation.

- ✍ Read 1 Corinthians 13: 4-8. Reflect for a minute what this verse means in applying it to caring for elderly parents.

   _____

   _____

   _____

   _____

The following story illustrates why it is often hard to care for the elderly and how we can put a "fresh" spin on how to look at the situation.

> My 100-year-old mother lives in a nursing home where others bathe, dress, and feed her. She rarely opens her eyes. When I visit, I tell her who I am and that I love her. Occasionally she responds but often she doesn't know me. I have wondered how I can get through to her. I want her to know that someone loves her and will see that her needs are met.
>
> One day I realized that in my relationship with God, I am often unaware that God is reaching out to me. God shows love for me and cares for my needs, but I am oblivious to God's gifts and unaware of the giver. Still, God is patient and keeps on giving!

Family Rivalry

Parents, siblings and in-laws can make unreasonable demands. There may be boundary problems if you answer "yes" to the following questions:

_____ Do you still react as you did when you were under parental authority?

_____ Do you give of your "treasures" out of guilt or fear?

_____ Are you resentful when you give of your "treasures"?

_____ Do you set limits out of desperation?

_____ Do you enable the family member's negative behavior?

A great tool for dealing with family rivalry is prayer. Pray for that person. God can even hear prayer when you are gritting your teeth! He understands how hard it is sometimes to pray for someone who is hurting you. Jesus was in so much agony when he prayed for his rivals that His sweat turned to blood. Yet he still prayed for those who turned against him.

Resolving Boundary Problems with Family

If you as an adult are not under guardians for a particular reason, you can and should make truly adult decisions. You are responsible for having control over your own will and are subject only to God the Father.

The Bible defines the transition into adulthood that we should all go through (being emotionally, physically, and financially independent of our parents). If we have not gone through the Biblical transition into adulthood and spiritual adoption into the family of God, boundary problems will continue.

Steps to take in resolving family boundary problems are:

1. Identify the conflict – discover what family boundary issue is being played out; prayerfully ask God to help you identify the true issue.

2. Identify the need that drives the conflict – this is about looking at your personal need! Is the need to be loved? Approved of? Accepted? Understood? Free to be yourself?

3. Take in and receive the good – humble yourself, reach out to a good Christian support system, and take in God's love.

4. Practice the boundary skills you are learning in this class – practice in situations where your boundaries will be honored and respected. Ask yourself who will honor your "no" and continue to love you unconditionally.

5. Say "no" to the bad – avoid hurtful situations; avoid those who abused and controlled you in the past until you are feeling stronger, then take a support person with you.

6. Forgive the aggressor – when you refuse to forgive someone, you still want something from that person and it keeps you tied to him or her forever. It is much better to receive grace from God, who has more than enough to give, and to forgive those who have no money to pay their debt with (Matthew 18: 21-35). In abusive situations, forgiving does not mean you have to have a relationship with that person.

Respond, Don't React

When you respond to what a family member says, you remain in control with options and choices. If you react, you may have boundary problems that need addressing.

When you react, the other person is in control. When you respond, you are in control.

> *"gentleness and self-control. Against such there is no law." Galatians 5:23*

A great response to judgmental statements is "I'll consider your opinion."

Loving Freely

Being motivated more by love than guilt frees you to see good boundaries in external family relationships. Because of God's perfect love, we can love and accept our imperfect families.

The person who has to remain forever in a protective mode is losing out on love and freedom.

As you continue to develop stronger boundaries with your family of origin and in-laws, remember that doing good for someone, when you freely choose to do it, is boundary enhancing.

> *"I give you a new commandment: love one another. As I have loved you, so you also should love one another." John 13:34-35*

Pick one family relationship that you are struggling with and write a prayer for that person each day in your journal for a week. As each day goes by, record after your prayer how you are feeling. At the end of the week, read what you have been writing, pay particular attention to how your feelings change.

Keeping Work Appropriate

Dealing with relationships in your chosen vocation.

In the book <u>Boundaries</u>, Drs. Cloud and Townsend write "Work is essentially good. It existed before the Fall. It was always part of God's plan for humanity to subdue and rule the earth (Genesis 1: 28)." *(Cloud, Boundaries: When to Say YES, When to Say NO, To Take Control of Your Life, 1992)*

The Biblical Perspective on Work

As a result of sin entering the world, God's plan for work changed (Genesis 3:17-19). Work became a labor of necessity which separated work from love for the world God had created for us to exist in. Rather than work being a desire to love and care for our environment, it became a mandatory task needed for survival. This shift in focus increases our wish to rebel, sparking our anger, and arousing our motivations to do the wrong thing (Romans 5:20, 4:15, 7:5).

Christians often have a warped perspective about work. Unless someone is working "in the ministry," work is usually considered to be secular. Work is usually defined by association with a paycheck. Work for women, however, is inclusive of being the CEO of a household!

✝ What is your perspective on your work? Do you consider it a ministry?

"Whatever you do, do fro the heart, as for the Lord and not for others,." Colossians. 3:23

✝ How could doing your work "as for the Lord" impact your attitudes and values about work?

In His parables, Jesus teaches a work ethic based on love under God. In your work, you reflect the image of God, who is Himself a worker, manager, developer, supervisor, and healer. This dispels the myth that ministry does not include the secular workplace.

A lack of boundaries creates problems in the workplace.

Getting Saddled with Another Person's Responsibilities

Favors and sacrifices done out of love are part of the Christian life. If your giving is helping the other person become better, you are following a Biblical principle. The Bible clearly says, however, that responsible action is required of the person who is on the receiving end of your loving help. If you do not see the other person being responsible after a reasonable period of time, set limits.

> *"[8]...and I shall cultivate the ground around it and fertilize it;[9] it may bear fruit in the future. If not, you can cut it down." Luke 13:8-9*

Working Too Much Overtime

Your job overload is your responsibility and your problem. You need to own the problem and do something about it. If you don't, you are playing the part of the victim.

✦ What does Matthew 10:14 tell you about setting limits in this type of situation?

Misplaced Priorities

Moses' father-in-law, Jethro, saw that Moses was going to wear himself out. Having limits will force you to prioritize and to work smart.

✦ Read Exodus 18:14-27 to see how Moses allowed good work to go too far.

✝ Establish a time budget for yourself by listing the various aspects of your work and assign the maximum amount of time you will spend with each.

Difficult Coworkers

The Law of Power says that you only have the power to change yourself. You cannot change another person! Focusing on the other person gives him or her power over you. You must refuse to allow that person to affect you.

The real problem lies in how you are relating to a difficult coworker. You must change your reactions to that person.

✦ Read Matthew 18:15-18. Discuss how these verses help in dealing with difficult coworkers.

When dealing with a difficult coworker, do the following:

- Examine your reactions and responses to him or her (be very specific).

- Make a list of how you can change your contact, interactions, and reactions to that person.

Critical Attitudes

You cannot change a critic. Allow those people to be who they are but keep yourself separate from them and do not internalize their opinion of you.

> *"7Whoever corrects the arrogant earns insults; and whoever reproves the wicked*
>
> *incurs opprobrium (harsh criticism or censure) 8Do not reprove the arrogant, lest they*
>
> *hate you; reprove the wise, and they will love you." Proverbs 9:7-8*

Ask yourself the following questions:

- What can you do to separate from them?

- What truths can you remind yourself of when you find yourself beginning to internalize a critic's words?

If you allow a critic to draw you in, thinking that you will change them, you are asking for trouble. **Don't get sucked into their game.**

Conflicts with Authority

When you experience strong feelings, see them as your responsibility. This leads you to work on any unfinished personal business and healing, as well as keeps you from acting irrationally toward co-workers and bosses.

> *"Am I now currying favor with human beings or God? Or am I seeking to please*
>
> *people? If I were still trying to please people, I would not be a slave of Christ."*
>
> *Galatians 1:10*

Ask yourself these questions:

- Whom does the person remind you of?

- Does their behavior remind you of the way a parent(s) or other family member treated you?

- How is the person's personality like your mother or father's?

- Are you being reminded of a competitive relationship from the past? If the answer is "yes", examine the similarities in your responses then and now.

Expecting Too Much of Work

Make sure you are meeting your needs for support and emotional repair outside of work. Protect your hurt places when you are in the workplace. The workplace is not set up to heal and may also wound unintentionally.

- What unrealistic expectations do you have for your work? Are you trying subconsciously to meet childhood needs?

- Where else can you turn—or are you turning—for nurturing, relationships, self-esteem, and approval?

- What is the problem with sharing your personal hurts with male co-workers?

  _____

- What danger is there in seeking counsel from co-workers you do not know very well?

  _____

"AN ATHEIST'S MOST EMBARRASSING MOMENT IS WHEN HE FEELS PROFOUNDLY THANKFUL FOR SOMETHING, BUT CAN'T THINK OF ANYBODY TO THANK FOR IT."

(MARY ANN VINCENT (1819-1887)

Taking Work-Related Stress Home

Set good boundaries for your work so that you can enjoy a healthy emotional life and a life that is in balance.

"You have been told, O mortal, what is good, and what the Lord requires of you: Only

to do justice and to love goodness, and to walk humbly with your God." Micah 6:8

Disliking Your Job

As you consider job possibilities, have a realistic expectation of yourself based on your own true self with your own particular gifts. You are to live up to God's expectations, not someone else's!

"Do not conform yourselves to this age but be transformed by the renewal of your mind, that you may discern what is the will of God, what is good and pleasing and perfect."

Romans 12:2

"Work is what we do to live—it should not give us identity or define the kind of person we are." (James, 2001)

✝ What will you do, in partnership with God, to find out who you really are and what kind of work you are made for? Take time to consider your dreams, loves, talents, and desires. These aspects (treasures) of yourself suggest the kind of work you would enjoy doing.

Finding Your Life's Work

Finding your life's work involves taking risks. God wants you to discover and use your gifts to His glory. He will hold you accountable for what you do. Look at your work as a partnership between you and God. He has given you gifts, and He wants you to develop them.

Commit your way to the Lord, and you will find your work identity and, with it, satisfaction.

✦ What promises do you find in Psalm 37:4-5?

✦ What warning do you find in Ecclesiastes 11:9?

Mentors are a very important part of finding your place in work related situations. Consider taking a church-led course in women mentoring women or talk to women's ministry leaders at your church for possible resources on learning about mentors or becoming a mentor yourself.

📖 In your journal, reflect for several days on the talents you believe you bring to your job. Write prayers of thanksgiving to God for this attributes. Continue reflecting in your journal and seeking God's true calling for you until we meet again.

lesson

Lesson 6

Appreciating the Beauty of a Woman

Dealing with boundaries in caring for yourself

What is Beautiful in God's Eyes?

The world tries to tell us what is beautiful about women. Let's build the **world's** ideal woman:

Hair color/length/style: _____

Eye Color: _____

Skin tone: _____

Height: _____ Weight: _____

Body shape: _____

Most popular personality type: _____

Most important physical aspect: _____

Most important intelligence skill: _____

Most important spiritual characteristic: _____

The world's idea of beauty is transient. It is in the eye of the beholder, relative to how we correlate it with what we believe and our mood at any given moment.

Now let's discover what God tells us about the ideal woman.

A woman is a result of God's direct handiwork. **God doesn't make junk and He doesn't make mistakes!** You are the dwelling place of the Holy Spirit, which makes you a temple befitting the King of all glory to dwell.

> *"2You are our letter, written on our hearts, known and read by all, 3shown to be a letter of Christ administered by us, written not in ink but by the Spirit of the living God, not on tables of stone but on tablets that are hearts of flesh."*
>
> *2 Corinthians 3:2-3*

✝ Is your beholder's eye in sync with what the world says or with what God says?
   Read 1 Corinthians 6: 19-20

A Holy Temple

Imagine you were zapped back in time and you land in front of Solomon's Temple in which resides the Ark of the Covenant (the most holy of places in the Old Testament stories).

The splendor of the temple was incredible. It took 30,000 laborers, 70,000 carriers, and 80,000 stonecutters at a minimum to complete the temple. No man, except for the high priest, could enter God's presence behind the curtain where the Ark resided.

In the New Testament, the curtain in the temple was ripped in two, symbolizing that through the blood of Jesus Christ, anyone may now have a personal relationship with God. Solomon's Temple exists no more but God still resides as the Holy Spirit in the temple which is **YOU**.

A woman's value is not the property value the world places on her but on the value God places on the temple where He resides!!

"There is so much beauty in a heart filled with the certainty that the Lord has once again come to fill, restore, and heal." (Troccoli, 1997)

Temple Housekeeping Tips

Most women have their "I'm going out to meet the world" dressing routine down. Is your routine similar to this?

- Clothes

- Hair

- Makeup

- Armor -- What!!??

According to Paul, we need to be dressed in the "full armor of God" before we are truly ready to face the world.

> *"Put on the armor of God so that you may be able to stand firm against the tactics of the devil." Ephesians 6:11*

✍ Look at the pieces of armor listed in Ephesians 6:14-17, and consider how each one helps you. Write a couple of thoughts that come to you.

I particularly like this translation of Ephesians 6:14-17 --

> *14 So then, take your stand! Fasten truth around your waist like a belt. Put on God's approval as your breastplate. 15 Put on your shoes so that you are ready to spread the Good News that gives peace. 16 In addition to all these, take the Christian faith as your shield. With it you can put out all the flaming arrows of the evil one. 17 Also take salvation as your helmet and the word of God as the sword that the Spirit supplies. (God's Word translation)*

✝ In light of this list, is there something you want to add to your routine?

Does God intend for you to not pay attention to your appearance? Absolutely not. Queen Esther was in a beauty contest that lasted a year! It just means you shouldn't make your appearance outside more important than your appearance inside. An entire book of the Bible would not have been devoted to Esther if she were not an example of a woman after God's own heart.

Women set on impressing others never impress God. In fact, it is one of the shortest routes to his displeasure. Purity of heart is what pleases God, not appearances.

How many women do you know (including yourself) that equate their beauty with what men think about them?

✞ Do you value what you think of your appearance or do you try to look a certain way for others?

The famous writer, Emily Dickinson, always dressed in white. Even a glimpse of her was rare, and gradually just the mention of her name brought shrugs and rolled eyes from her neighbors. After her death, they found the stacks of poems that lined her room—poems that revealed her literary genius and touched millions. No one had ever imagined the creative force driving her life with such passion. No one, not even her family, knew the well within her that served such rare wine.

Most women are familiar with the story of Mary and Martha. (The story is told in all four gospels: Matthew 26:6-13, Mark 14:1-9, Luke 10-38-42, and John 11:1 – 12:3.)

What is remembered most about Mary is that she sat at Jesus' feet while her sister Martha "slaved away" in the kitchen. We honor her for what she does but seldom for who she is.

✍ Write some descriptive words about "who" Mary was.

The most overlooked verse in this story can be read in Mark 14:9 --

"Amen, I say to you, wherever the gospel is proclaimed to the whole world, what she has done will be told in memory of her."

What did Jesus promise? The fulfillment of the promise is that we still hear her story today!

Jesus calls us to recognize and treasure the "Mary" in us or other women. Mary was a single woman; we don't know if it was by choice, destiny, divorce, or death. Failing to see the passion she has for the Lord that drives her life may cause you to think of her as different.

Do you have a Martha you know at church or who works with you? Her life is spent:

1. Caring for aging parents

2. Teaching children
3. Fighting battles on behalf of the poor, the dispossessed, and the victims of our culture
4. Interceding and bringing others to Jesus through her witness

Hers is not a romantic life or maybe it is; daily faithfulness which leads to priceless romancing by the Savior!

Money, Money!

Many women feel valued by the material possessions they have. They only feel secure if there is a large sum in the bank account.

How much is enough?

> *"Where there are great riches, there are also many to devour them. Of what use are*
>
> *they to the owner except as a feast for the eyes along. Ecclesiastes 5:10*

Paul says the wellbeing we long for will never come from money but from inside our souls when godliness is united with contentment.

> *"But the one who is self-indulgent is dead while she lives." 1 Timothy 6:6*

The Worth of a Woman

Anytime you feel diminished or accused of being unworthy, those are Satan's words. Jesus said in Revelations 12:10 that Satan is "the accuser of our brothers." We can recognize his creepy voice anytime we feel accused.

The Holy Spirit woos us, loves us, and moves us to a place of understanding. He never undermines us, his children, with derogatory messages that make us feel worthless. We are worth the price of Jesus on the cross, which makes us acceptable to a holy God just as you are.

Let's revisit your woman on page one of this lesson and build God's ideal woman.

Hair color/length/style:_____

Eye Color: _____

Skin tone: _____

Height: _____ Weight: _____

Body shape: _____

Most popular personality type: _____

Most important physical aspect: _____

Most important intelligence skill: _____

Most important spiritual characteristic: _____

✝ What did you learn about your worth as a woman growing up? (These are messages that were told to you or you learned by watching female role models.)

✝ How have these beliefs worked well for you as an adult woman? How have these beliefs hurt you as an adult woman?

Boundaries are about balance. When you consider your physical, mental, and spiritual worth, know where the right boundaries are. Measure them by God's standards, not the world's.

Enjoy being female, care about your health and appearance. That is ok! You are God's temple. Remember, however, that He dwells inside and make sure the inside of your temple is a holy, pure home for the Holy Spirit. You are the love of God's life and He delights in you!

📖 Each day write in your journal something positive about yourself according to what God says. Pray for God to reinforce these beliefs and for the Holy Spirit's guidance as you put on your Spiritual armor as part of your morning routine.

Avoiding Church Lady Syndrome

Dealing with boundaries in volunteer relationships

Why do you over commit in volunteer areas?

Some commitment areas in our lives are "musts" but others are ones we chose freely. In God's family, there are many areas of service but not all persons have the gifts to serve in each area. It is difficult to be in a position that you have committed to but are always reluctant to be active in.

Why doesn't your "no" work when you are asked to take on another task in the Christian body of believers? Consider the following three reasons:

1. We are our own worst enemies. It is easier to set limits on other people than it is to set limits on ourselves.

    Paul struggled in this area. Read *Romans 7:15-19*; can you identify with Paul's internal struggles?

    [15]What I do, I do not understand. For I do not do what I want, but I do what I hate. [16]Now if I do what I do not want, I concur that the law is good. [17]So now it is no anger I who do it, but sin that dwells in me. [18]For I know that good does not dwell in me, that is, in my flesh. The willing is ready at hand, but doing the good is not. [19]For I do not do the good I want, but I do the evil I do not want."

2. We try to use will power to solve our boundary problems. We make a vow to God and ourselves that we will say "no" next time. If all we need is our will to overcome evil, we certainly don't need a Savior.

    Our will is strengthened by relationship—the power of the relationship promised in the Cross. Saint Paul tells us in his First Letter to the Corinthians:

"For Christ did not send me to baptize but to preach the gospel, and not with the wisdom of human eloquence, so that the cross of Christ might not be emptied of its meaning." 1 Corinthians 1:17

3. We tend to isolate ourselves when our boundary issue deals with what we consider to be a spiritual issue. You might be saying "How can I tell someone I resent serving at church in a particular capacity? They will think I'm not a servant of the Lord."

    Since the Fall in the Garden, our human instinct has been to withdraw from relationship when we are in trouble, when we most need other people.

    "He answered, 'I heard you in the garden; but I was afraid, because I was naked, so I hid.'" Genesis 3:10

    You can't solve your boundary problems in a vacuum. The more you isolate, the harder the struggle becomes.

    ✍ What do the images of the vine (John 15:1-5) and the body (Ephesians 4:16) and the instruction of James 5:16 teach about the importance of being connected to God and his people as you confront your self-boundary problems?

Commitment Inventory

Evaluate where you are serving for God:

✟ How many acts of "service" do you feel obligated to perform?

✟ How many "ministries" are you working in so that you can feel good about yourself as a giving, Christian woman?

✟ How much are you resenting those women who seem to be rested, refreshed, and more in tune with God than you are?

✟ Are you more Martha or more Mary? More business or more blessing?

Spiritual Stress Test

When was the last time you had your inner heart checked? Perhaps you are about due for a spiritual stress test to measure its overall health. To assist, I am providing you with several cardiograms to chart your heartbeat under varying conditions. The first graph is a sample to help you see how it works. Let's see how strong or weak your spiritual pulse is under each category.

SAMPLE: Finances

Give Generously	Give Regularly	Save Wisely	Live within My Means	Content with What I Have

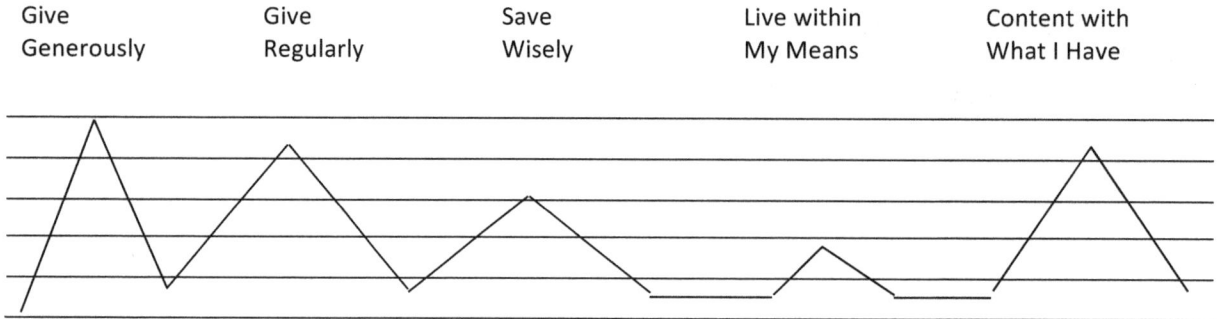

> ✍ Now…you complete the finance category and the others for yourself.

FINANCES

Give Generously	Give Regularly	Save Wisely	Live within My Means	Content with What I Have

HOME

Put Others First	Patience with Spouse	Pray Regularly	Model Christ	Family Devotions

WORK

Honest	Good Attitude	Servant to Others	Respect Authority	Initiate Ideas

_____
_____
_____
_____
_____
_____

FRIENDS

Loyal	Truthful	Give Comfort	Forgiving	Encouraging

_____
_____
_____
_____
_____
_____

ENEMIES

Kind	Pray for Them	Refuse to Gossip	Ready to Forgive	Honest with Yourself

_____
_____
_____
_____
_____
_____

GOD

Bible Study	Prayer	Worship	Witnessing	Good Samaritan Lifestyle

_____
_____
_____
_____
_____
_____

"I want to serve the Lord, though!" you say. That is good but where should you be serving? Let's try to figure out how God designed you specifically to further His kingdom.

> "[6]*Since we have gifts that differ according to the grace given to us, let us exercise them: if prophecy, in proportion to the faith;* [7]*if ministry, in ministering; if one is a teacher, in teaching;* [8]*if one exhorts, in exhortation; if one contributes, in generosity; if one is over others, with diligence; if one does acts of mercy, with cheerfulness."*
> Romans 12:6-8

These gifts shape our personality, are built into us, and are part of us. Since they provide the reason for why we do what we do, they are called **motivational gifts**.

The motivational gifts are defined as:

- **Mercy** – showing compassion, love and caring
- **Teaching** – researching and communicating the truth
- **Service** – serving or doing for others
- **Giving** – finding the resources
- **Prophesy** – clearly perceiving the will of God
- **Exhortation** – encouraging others
- **Administration** – organizing, leading or directing
- ✍ Turn to the Appendix in the back of the book and complete the Motivational Gifts inventory.

A second type of gift is called a **ministry gift**. Ministry gifts are listed in the great Pauline letter about the church.

> *"And he gave some as apostles, others prophets, others as evangelists, others as pastors and teachers,"* Ephesians 4:11

These type of gifts are the ways that we *use* our motivational gifts in service so that the Church can function as Christ's representative on earth. The five ministry gifts are not titles for church staff members but the functions of all believers.

The third type of gift is called a **manifestation gift**.

Manifestation gifts are listed in *1 Corinthians 12:7-10* and are supernatural expressions given by the Holy Spirit.

These gifts are not controlled by our will but are given to the person who is being ministered to in order to reveal a deeper understanding of God.

Using Our Gifts Correctly

As we understand the nature of the gifts, we can understand why we feel the way we do about certain things and why we respond to others the way we do. Each one of the gifts come with strengths that are displayed as we allow the Holy Spirit to work through us as well as weaknesses that result from the misuse of the gifts as we attempt to live on our own apart from the Spirit's empowerment.

When we are working within the scope of our giftedness, we find that we are energized and find amazing strength and competence. Our passion for life increases because we are functioning in the realm God intended for us through the power of the Holy Spirit. When we try to work in those areas that God has not gifted us to work in, we have a tendency toward burnout and disillusionment. As long as we allow the Spirit to move within us in our area of giftedness, there is no limit to what God will be able to accomplish.

📖 Write thoughts and prayers in your journal about what you have discovered in this list asking God to show you where he wants you to use your special gifts. If you are struggling in an area where you have over committed or have committed in the wrong area, write your thoughts about what you need to do to correct these situations.

Understanding God's Plan in Abusive Relationships

Setting boundaries with abusive spouses

What is Marriage?

God formally instituted marriage and only He has the right to do so. God has revealed His will in the Bible. Men and women can marry, be divorced, and be remarried only if, when, and how God says they may without sinning.

> *"That is why a man leaves his father and mother and clings to his wife, and the two of them become one body." Genesis 2:24*

Marriage is a foundational institution. Marriage is a covenantal relationship of vital importance in the church. The church is where God's special foundation for relationships rests. Marriage is considered a sub-unit residing on the foundation.

The church as a special covenantal community becomes weakened as the special unit known as marriage weakens. Let's think of marriages as "houses" for a minute and what happens when a" house" or "household" is weakened. The attack on marriage is an attack on the basic sub-unit of the church.

The following examples demonstrate that God sees households as a single unit according to the Bible.

> *"Then the Lord said to Noah: Go into the ark, you and all your **household**, for you alone in this generation have I found to be righteous before me." Genesis 7:1*

> *"Should any of them pass outside the doors of your house, their blood will be on their own heads, and we will be guiltless. But if **anyone in your house** is harmed, their blood will be on our heads." Joshua 2:19*

*"And they said, 'Believe in the Lord Jesus and you and your **household** will be saved." Acts 16:31*

The Covenant of Companionship

The reason for marriage is to solve the problem of loneliness. Companionship is the essence of marriage.

This does not mean that single people have to lead lonely lives. God has called some to be exceptions and provides for their need for companionship by gifting them especially to lead the single life. Many Christian singles are sad and lonely because they have not tested their gifts to determine whether or not they have been granted the special gift of "single service" for Christ's empire.

Companionship involves closeness. A companion is someone you enter into a close union or relationship with. You are intimately united in:

- thoughts

- goals, plans

- efforts

- physically (sexual union)

What does "helper mean in God design for marriage?

> *"[18]The Lord God said: It is not good for the man to be alone. I will make a helper suited to him. [24]That is why a man leaves his father and mother and clings to his wife, and the two o them become one body."*

In older versions of the Bible, the term was used instead of "helper." Helpmeet is a hybrid (mixed) word that has been adapted in the English language. There were two distinct words: *help* meant exactly what our present-day word *helper* means and *meet* meant *appropriate to, corresponding to* or *approximating at every point*. This means the woman is the other half—not better half or worse half! She approximates (close to being like) her husband.

As her husband's counterpart (complement of), the woman completes or fills out the man's life, making him a larger person than he could have been alone, bringing into his frame of reference a new feminine dimension from which to view life that he could have known in no other way.

The husband in turn brings a masculine perspective that enlarges the wife's life. A marriage companion according to God's design is someone you can:

- talk things over with

- be accountable with

- care for

- share joys, perplexities, ideas, fears, sorrows and disappointments

- be a helper to

Paul explained companionship in marriage by saying:

> [28]*So [also] husbands should love their wives as their own bodies. He who loves his wife loves himself.* [29]*For no one hates his own flesh but rather nourishes and cherishes it, even as Christ does the church,* [30]*because we are members of his body."*
> *Ephesians 5:28-30*

✝ Marriage is intimate and designed to be a functioning unit. What is Paul saying in Ephesians 5:28-30?

When Marriage Becomes a Dictatorship

Abuse in marriages takes many forms: physical, emotional, mental, and spiritual. Many women come to the point where they cannot discern if they are being compliant in their marriage out of fear or submission. If children are involved, the desire to protect their children adds another aspect to an already complicated question.

Sometimes women enable their husbands to be dictators for two different reasons:

- Some women fear their own influence and power—woman grew up in a home where her opinion was not valued; out of habit or fear she continues in adulthood to defer to her husband.
- Some women have an untrue understanding of Biblical submission – God designed the husband to be the head of the household but that does not mean the wife surrenders her influence.

"When drastic perversions of leadership occur—like abuse, addiction and gross immorality—a godly woman must temporarily take "the driver's seat" in order to prevent the calamity." (Slattery, 2001)

    ✎ The Old Testament story of Abigail is an illustration of a wife who rightly refused to

        follow her husband's immoral leadership. Read 1 Samuel 25:3.

        How is Abigail described?

        How is Nabal described?

Abigail was not submissive to her husband in this story. She took action against what her husband wanted because his foolish behaviors almost lead to the death of their entire family.

- **A wife should not behave in a sinful manner, even if her husband tells her to:**

"..there is no authority except from God." Romans 13:1

God gives a husband's authority to him and he is under God's authority; when a husband asks his wife to do something that is clearly sinful, God vetoes his authority. For example:

- Watching a pornographic movie (she should refuse)

- Tells her to lie (she should not)

- Forbids her to go to church (she should still go)

- Tells her to treat her parents in a dishonorable way (she must not submit)

- **A wife should protect the dignity of all in her household.**

Scripture is very clear about the value and dignity of each human life. All humans are commanded to treat each other with love and kindness—

"Finally, all of you, be of one mind, sympathetic, loving toward one another,

compassionate, humble." 1 Peter 3:8.

Jesus was a strong champion of the dignity of others; particularly those that were abused by society. (See John 8 for the story of the woman caught in adultery.)

Fathers, in particular, are placed in the role of protecting their children physically, emotionally, and spiritually. When a man abuses his position of power and authority to

---

communicate destructive messages to his children, his wife must step in to protect and reaffirm the dignity of those in her home. Defending a child from an angry or abusive spouse can still be done in the spirit of respect. How could you respond to a spouse who says the following to a child of yours:

✞ You are a failure.

✞ You are stupid and will never amount to anything.

- **A wife should protect the dignity of all in her personhood.**

  When a husband humiliates his wife emotionally, socially, and sexually, he is robbing her of the worth and dignity with which she was created. Allowing this to occur should never be confused with submission.

  Scripture teaches a Christian who has accepted Christ as their savior is a temple of the Holy Spirit (II Corinthians 6:16). You should never allow anyone to rip apart and vandalize your mind, soul, or body.

- **A wife should not enable her husband to live in sin.**

  You should not try to *control* the conduct of your husband; however, you do play an active role in *responding* to his behavior. If a woman supports her husband's sinful lifestyle, the natural consequences will likely affect and harm the entire family. See *Joshua 7* for a story that illustrates the damage enabling sin can bring about.

  If you try to "nag" at your husband about his sinful lifestyle, the less he will listen. Often he will become more involved in the lifestyle to prove his wife has no control over him. In *1 Peter 3*, Peter tells wives to influence their husbands through a "gentle and quiet spirit."

  A wife's ultimate goal is to help her husband clearly see the destructive choices he is making. When a woman uses her influence this way, her husband is clearly placed in the role of making his own decision. **She takes herself out of the equation**.

Bitterness and Resentment

Many abused women find themselves falling into negative feelings due to their disappointment over broken marriages. All of the dreams of marriage and family life have been ripped to shreds and they feel cheated of life's promises.

The book of Ruth in the Bible is often overlooked as a great source of information to women on the topic of bitterness. The main character is Ruth but an important person to also study in this book is Naomi, a woman who suffers many losses in her family unit.

Naomi becomes bitter over the loss of her husband and sons.

"But she said to them 'Do not call me Naomi [Sweet]. Call me Mara [Bitter], for the Almighty has made my life very bitter.'" Ruth 1:20

Life had not been kind to Naomi and she resented it.

"I went away full, but the Lord has brought me back empty. Why should you call me 'Sweet,' since the Lord has brought me to trial, and the Almighty has pronounced evil sentence on me." Ruth 1:21

Despite her feelings towards God, however, Naomi does not allow her bitterness and anger to consume her. She expresses and vents her feelings but she does not give up.

✝ Do you allow the kindness of others to give you hope? (A stranger opens a door for you; someone offers you a seat on the bus; someone smiles at you for no apparent reason; a beautiful bird flies by your window; a song of encouragement lifts your spirits.)

Naomi seizes her hope and turns it into action. The Lord did not abandon or afflict Naomi in her hardships. He becomes the supreme redeemer, generous and kind, compassionate and comforting. If Naomi had given in to the temptation to withdraw, withhold, and withstand the possibility for God to restore and bless her, then she would have missed a joy richer and deeper than the losses she suffered.

If you are experiencing abuse in your marriage, seek the counsel of your pastor and a counselor who holds the same Christian beliefs. Do not let your life become one of bitterness and struggle.

📖 Carefully pray over the information you have learned and take action if in an abusive relationship. If you know of another woman who could use the information, pray with her and share your knowledge learned in this chapter.

Appendix

Spiritual Gifts Inventory

This inventory provides some general characteristics of the seven motivational gifts. It is designed to provide you with an instrument for producing a profile of your own spiritual gift. This can be combined with your personal experience and interests for a complete picture. The inventory consists of forty-nine items. Some items reflect concrete actions; other items are descriptive of traits; and still others are statements of belief or value.

Directions: As you read each item, decide whether the sentence is true or descriptive of you. Circle the number to the right of the sentence that most accurately reflects your decision. Your first response to the question is usually the best. (If you are viewing this book electronically, use a piece of paper to record your answers.)

1. Not at all, this is untrue for me.
2. Occasionally, this is true of me about 25 percent of the time.
3. Frequently, this describes me about 50 percent of the time.
4. Most of the time this would describe me.
5. Highly characteristic, this is definitely true for me.

1. I want to measure everything by God's word.	1	2	3	4	5
2. Others seem to look to me for advice and help.	1	2	3	4	5
3. I am bothered by others' lack of compassion.	1	2	3	4	5
4. I enjoy discussing ideas and issues.	1	2	3	4	5
5. I can usually visualize the final result of a major project.	1	2	3	4	5
6. Remembering the likes and dislikes of others is easy for me.	1	2	3	4	5
7. My financials resources are above average.	1	2	3	4	5
8. I dominate conversations with detail others don't care about.	1	2	3	4	5
9. Injustices and evil in the world trouble me.	1	2	3	4	5
10. Setting and achieving goals is important to me.	1	2	3	4	5
11. People see me as a frank and outspoken person.	1	2	3	4	5
12. Discouraged people are encouraged by my words.	1	2	3	4	5
13. I often neglect my own work in order to help others.	1	2	3	4	5
14. I find it easy to identify with the feelings of others.	1	2	3	4	5
15. In helping people, I seem to know the right thing to do.	1	2	3	4	5
16. I enjoy doing little things to help people.	1	2	3	4	5
17. My natural tendency is to step up and take control.	1	2	3	4	5
18. My life is an open book for others to see.	1	2	3	4	5
19. It's natural for me to show kindness to people.	1	2	3	4	5
20. I will tell people if I think they're doing wrong.	1	2	3	4	5
21. When a question about truth comes up, I am usually right.	1	2	3	4	5
22. I like to tell people what's important to me.	1	2	3	4	5
23. People learn easily from me.	1	2	3	4	5

24. Possessions are meant to be shared.	1	2	3	4	5
25. I don't expect repayment for favors I do for others.	1	2	3	4	5
26. I'm a good counselor.	1	2	3	4	5
27. Communicating the facts in a situation is something I do well.	1	2	3	4	5
28. I am a task oriented person.	1	2	3	4	5
29. I find it easy to maintain an optimistic outlook.	1	2	3	4	5
30. I enjoy being responsible for the success of the group.	1	2	3	4	5
31. I will stand alone on something I believe in strongly.	1	2	3	4	5
32. I am a task oriented person.	1	2	3	4	5
33. Doing things for people in need makes me happy.	1	2	3	4	5
34. It's not important for others to know the good things I do.	1	2	3	4	5
35. I have an urge to tell others about my life in Christ.	1	2	3	4	5
36. I can usually think clearly in confusion.	1	2	3	4	5
37. I am attracted to people who are hurting.	1	2	3	4	5
38. Deadlines challenge me and I usually meet them on time.	1	2	3	4	5
39. My convictions are absolute with no room for compromise.	1	2	3	4	5
40. I enjoy investing in the ministries of other people.	1	2	3	4	5
41. I find strength from bearing other's burdens.	1	2	3	4	5
42. My use of knowledge may appear prideful.	1	2	3	4	5
43. I like to see all the pieces of a problem come together.	1	2	3	4	5
44. I can find the best resources to meet specific needs.	1	2	3	4	5
45. I often volunteer my time and talents to worthwhile causes.	1	2	3	4	5
46. Others seeking direction in life will look to me for guidance.	1	2	3	4	5
47. I usually select the best person for a particular task.	1	2	3	4	5
48. My focus on right and wrong may be read as being judgmental.	1	2	3	4	5
49. I enjoy helping others develop a plan of action to deal with their concerns.	1	2	3	4	5

PROPHECY

DEFINITION / CHARACTERISTICS

The supernatural ability to declare the truth of God, especially as it applies to an immediate situation among the people of God or in society as a whole. Prophecy occasionally has to do with the future, but primarily speaks to the present situation. Romans 12:6, Luke 7:24-28.

NATURE OF GOD

The God who confronts sin.

HOW USED IN THE BODY

Their goal is bringing persons face-to-face with God. They discern and reveal motives and actions, have strong convictions, and a need to express them verbally.

MISUSES / MISUNDERSTANDINGS

Frankness may be viewed as harshness. Focus on right and wrong may be judged as intolerance of partial good. Efforts to gain results may be seen as using gimmicks. Public boldness and strict standards may hinder intimate personal relationships.

CHARACTERISTICS

Item Number	1	9	11	21	31	39	48	Total Score
Score								_____

SERVING

The supernatural ability to identify ad meet practical needs in the body of Christ. They work best short-term, alone, and tend to do things quickly. Romans 12:7; Titus 3:14

NATURE OF GOD
The God who sent Jesus.

HOW USED IN THE BODY
This person is aware and motivated to help with tasks or projects which will go undone unless someone pitches in. They see needs and enjoy responding.

MISUSES / MISUNDERSTANDINGS
Insistence on serving may appear to be rejection of being served. Quickness in meeting needs may appear to be pushy. Their disregard for personal needs may extend to their own family's needs.

Item Number	6	13	15	16	28	32	45	Total Score
Score								————

TEACHING

DEFINITION / CHARACTERISTICS

The supernatural ability to research and communicate truth in such a way that others will learn and understand the truth. They communicate the truth with obvious results, and tend to work systematically and with accuracy. They are usually very interested in details. Romans 12:7, Acts 18:24-28

NATURE OF GOD

The God who gave his Word.

HOW USED IN THE BODY

They enjoy research in order to validate truth, and they have the ability to present this truth in a systematic sequence. Their teaching generally produces results in those that hear.

MISUSES / MISUNDERSTANDINGS

The emphasis on the accuracy of scriptural interpretation may appear to neglect its practical application. The concern to impart details of research may appear to be unnecessary to those listening. They may appear to be boring and too interested in details.

Item Number	4	8	22	23	27	36	42	Total Score
Score								———

EXHORTATION

DEFINITION / CHARACTERISTICS

The supernatural ability to minister words of encouragement, comfort, challenge, and counsel to members of the body. Problems are only challenges, and they are drawn to those seeking spiritual growth. They have a desire to visualize specific achievement and prescribe steps of action. Romans 12:8, Hebrews 10:25

NATURE OF GOD

The God who sends His Spirit.

HOW USED IN THE BODY

Their gift is usually exercised one-on-one, but may be exercised publicly. Learning and teaching practical information is their desire. People tend to fee good around them.

MISUSES / MISUNDERSTANDINGS

The emphasis on steps of action may appear to oversimplify the problem. The desire to win non-Christians through living examples may appear as a lack of interest in personal evangelism.

Item Number	2	12	20	26	29	46	49	Total Score
Score								————

GIVING

DEFINITION / CHARACTERISTICS
The supernatural ability to contribute one's material resources to the needs of others, and to the work of the Lord in a sensitive, effective, generous, and cheerful manner. They contribute sacrificially. Romans 12:8, Mark 12:41-44

NATURE OF GOD
The God who creates.

HOW USED IN THE BODY
They can see needs that others may not, and their giving motivates other people. They tend to shun pressure and publicity and enjoy giving behind the scenes.

MISUSES / MISUNDERSTANDINGS
The desire to increase the effectiveness of a ministry by his/her gift may appear as an attempt to control the work or the person. The desire to deal with large sums of money may appear to be a focus on temporal values.

Item Number	7	18	24	34	35	40	44	Total Score
Score								————

ADMINISTRATION

DEFINITION / CHARACTERISTICS

The supernatural ability to organize and direct the tasks which need to be accomplished, getting the work done with and through the labors of others. They lead people and communicate so they perform to harmoniously reach goals for god's purposes. Romans 12:8, Acts 6:1-7

NATURE OF GOD

The God who rules.

HOW USED IN THE BODY

They enjoy being the leader and can endure adverse reactions to get the job done. They tend to assume responsibility if no structured leadership exist. There is an ability to see the overall picture and clarify long-range goals.

MISUSES / MISUNDERSTANDINGS

The ability to delegate responsibility may appear as laziness in avoiding work. The willingness to endure reaction may appear as callousness. The viewing of people as resources may appear that projects are more important than people.

Item Number	5	10	17	30	38	43	47	Total Score
Score								_____

MERCY

The supernatural ability to manifest genuine empathy, compassion, and cheerful love toward individuals who suffer from many different problems. They have a strong desire to remove hurts and bring healing to others. Roans 12:8, Luke 10:33-35

The God who redeems.

They have a sensitivity to words and actions which will hurt other people, and there is an ability to discern sincere motives in others. There is an attraction to and an understanding of people who are in distress.

The avoidance of firmness may appear to be weakness and indecisiveness. The sensitivity to words and actions which cause hurt may appear to be taking up another's offense.

Item Number	3	14	19	25	33	37	41	Total Score
Score								———

Summary of Gifts

Gift	Score
Prophecy	____
Serving	____
Teaching	____
Exhortation	____
Giving	____
Administration	____
Mercy	____

After you have recorded your score for each gift from the inventory, circle the gift with the highest score. When you combine this with your personal experience and assessment of yourself, and with the feedback from others, you can ten identify your primary motivational gift.

Using Motivational Gifts

A family group is eating together for a celebration. One of the children drops ice cream on the floor. If each of the seven gifts were represented in the family, here is what each might say:

Prophecy – "That what happens when you don't pay attention to what you're doing." (Motivation: To correct)

Serving – "Here, let me help you clean it up." (Motivation: To fulfill a need)

Teaching – "The reason that fell is that it was to heavy on one side." (Motivation: To discover why it happened)

Exhortation – "Next time, let's serve the dessert in a bigger bowl." (Motivation: To correct the future)

Giving – "I'll be happy to get some more ice cream." (Motivation: To give to a tangible need)

Administration – "Bill, would you get the mop. Doris, please help pick it up and help me fix some other dessert." (Motivation: Organizing others to correct a problem)

Mercy – "Don't be upset. It could have happened to anyone, I've done worse." (Motivation: To relieve embarrassment)

Bibliography

Cloud, H. &. (1992). *Boundaries: When to Say YES, When to Say NO, To Take Control of Your Life.* Michigan: Zondervan Publishing House.

Cloud, H. &. (2002). *Boundaries in Marriage.* Michigan: Zondervan Publishing House.

James, K. C. (2001). *What I Wish I'd Known Before I Go Married.* Multnomah.

Lotz, A. G. (1997). *God's Story.* Dallas: Word Publishing.

Slattery, J. (2001). *Finding the Hero in Your Husband, Surrendering the Way God Intended.* Florida: Health Communications, Inc.

Troccoli, K. (1997). *My Life is in Your Hands.* Zondervan Publishing Company.

Young, S. (2004). *Jesus Calling.* Thomas Nelson.

www.ingramcontent.com/pod-product-compliance
Lightning Source LLC
Chambersburg PA
CBHW081522040426
42447CB00013B/3307